Student Interactive

# myView

## L I T E R A C Y

**1**

**SAVVAS**

LEARNING COMPANY

**SAVVAS**
LEARNING COMPANY

ISBN-13: 978-0-134-90875-5
ISBN-10:　　0-134-90875-9

10　22

Julie Coiro, Ph.D.

Jim Cummins, Ph.D.

Pat Cunningham, Ph.D.

Elfrieda Hiebert, Ph.D.

Pamela Mason, Ed.D.

Ernest Morrell, Ph.D.

P. David Pearson, Ph.D.

Frank Serafini, Ph.D.

Alfred Tatum, Ph.D.

Sharon Vaughn, Ph.D.

Judy Wallis, Ed.D.

Lee Wright, Ed.D.

# My Neighborhood

**UNIT 1**

# My Neighborhood

## Essential Question

### What is a neighborhood?

▶ **Watch**

**"Welcome to My Neighborhood"** See what you can learn about a neighborhood.

🦉 **TURN and TALK** What can you see in a neighborhood?

**SAVVAS realize™**

Go ONLINE for all lessons.

- ▶ VIDEO
- 🔊 AUDIO
- 🎮 GAME
- ✏️ ANNOTATE
- 📖 BOOK
- 🔍 RESEARCH

## Spotlight on Realistic Fiction

### Reading-Writing Bridge

- Academic Vocabulary
- Read Like a Writer, Write for a Reader
- Spelling • Language and Conventions

### Writing Workshop

- Writing Club • Digital Tools We Can Use Together
- Making and Responding to Suggestions
- Asking and Answering Questions • Publish and Celebrate

### Project-Based Inquiry

- Inquire • Research • Collaborate

Read Together

# Independent Reading

In this unit, you will read books with your teacher. You will also select, or choose, books to read on your own.

## How to Find a Just-Right Book:

Select a book. Open to any page. Start reading.

Put one finger up for each word you do not know. Use the chart below.

| 0–1 | The book is too easy. |
|---|---|
| 2–3 | The book is just right. |
| 4 | The book is okay to try. |
| 5 or more | The book is too hard. |

Should you read the book?    Yes    No

# My Reading Log

| Date | Book | Pages Read | Minutes Read | My Ratings |
|------|------|------------|--------------|------------|
| | | | | 😊 😐 ☹️ |
| | | | | 😊 😐 ☹️ |
| | | | | 😊 😐 ☹️ |
| | | | | 😊 😐 ☹️ |
| | | | | 😊 😐 ☹️ |

You may wish to use a Reader's Notebook to record and respond to your reading.

# Unit Goals

In this unit, you will

- read realistic fiction
- write a story
- learn about neighborhoods

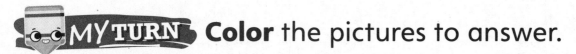 **Color** the pictures to answer.

| | 👍 | 👎 |
|---|---|---|
| I can read realistic fiction. | | |
| I can make and use words to read and write realistic fiction. | | |
| I can write a story. | | |
| I understand what a neighborhood is. | | |

# Academic Vocabulary

| type | group | settle | various |
|------|-------|--------|---------|

In this unit, you will learn about **various types** of neighborhoods where **groups** of people live. These people choose to **settle** in a neighborhood.

**MY TURN** Complete the chart with a check mark.

|         | I know the word | I don't know the word |
|---------|-----------------|-----------------------|
| type    |                 |                       |
| group   |                 |                       |
| settle  |                 |                       |
| various |                 |                       |

# Neighbor to Neighbor

**TURN and TALK** Sometimes we want to learn more about interesting topics, so we ask questions for informal inquiry. What questions do you have about the information here?

## Little Libraries

Some neighborhoods have free outdoor libraries. Anyone can borrow a book from the box.

## Colorful Meals

Some neighbors help people get healthy food. Children make colorful placemats.

## How can neighbors help each other?

# Furry Friends

Some dogs sit with children who are learning to read. You can train your dog to help too!

# Middle Sounds

 **SEE and SAY** Every word has at least one vowel sound. Say each picture name. Listen to the middle sound. Then say the middle sound.

# Short a

Short **a** is often spelled **a**, as in **map**.

 **MY TURN** Say each picture name. Write **a** if the word has the short **a** sound.

# Short a

 **MY TURN** Draw a picture of something with the short **a** sound. Write the letter that spells that sound.

_____

---------------

_____

**MY TURN** Say each picture name. Write the vowel that spells the middle sound.

_____

---------------

_____

_____

---------------

_____

# Short a

**MY TURN** Say each picture name. Write the letter that spells the middle sound.

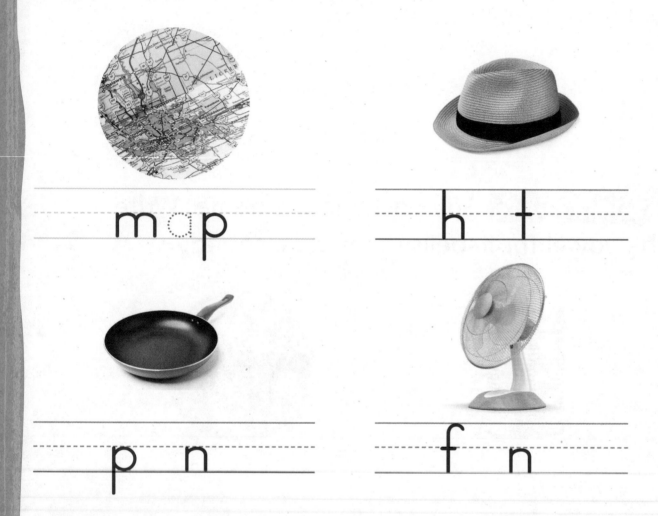

m a p

h ___ t

p ___ n

f ___ n

**MY TURN** Write **a** to finish the words in the sentence.

T ___ m ___ is a ___ c ___ t.

# Alliteration

**SEE and SAY** Sometimes groups of words begin with the same initial sound. Say the picture names. Tell the sound that is the same in each picture name.

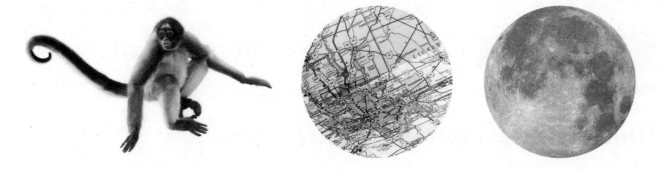

## Mm, Ss, Tt

The letter **m** makes the **m** sound in **mat**.
The letter **s** makes the **s** sound in **sat**.
The letter **t** makes the **t** sound in **tap**.

**MY TURN** Read these words.

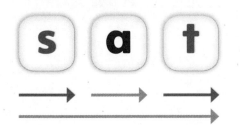

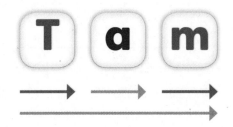

**Read Together**

# My Words to Know

Some words you must remember and practice.

**MY TURN** Read the words.

| a | I | is | his | see |
|---|---|----|-----|-----|

**MY TURN** Complete the sentences with words from the box. Read the sentences.

**Handwriting** Print the words clearly.

1. _____ am Tam.

2. I _____ Sam.

3. Sam _____ at _____ mat.

4. I am at _____ mat.

# Mm, Ss, Tt

**TURN and TALK** Read these words with a partner.

| am | Sam | Tam |
|----|-----|-----|
| at | sat | mat |

**MY TURN** Write **m**, **s**, or **t** to finish the words.

1. Sam ___sa___ .

2. Is Sam at a ___a___ ?

**TURN and TALK** Read the sentences.

# Mm, Ss, Tt

 **MY TURN** Say each picture name. Write **m**, **s**, or **t** to finish each word.

Listen to the first sound of the picture name.

m a n

_ a g

_ a t

_ a d

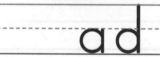 **MY TURN** Write a word you wrote to finish the sentence.

Sam is at a _____ .

# At a Mat

I am Tam.

I see Sam.

AUDIO

Audio with Highlighting

ANNOTATE

Read the story. Highlight the five words with the short **a** sound.

I see a <u>mat</u>.

Sam is at his mat.

**Underline** the three words
with the **t** sound.

I sat at a mat.

Sam sat at his mat.

**Highlight** the three words
with the **s** sound.

23

**My Learning Goal**

I can read realistic fiction.

SPOTLIGHT ON GENRE

# Realistic Fiction

Realistic fiction is a made-up story that could happen in real life. It has characters, or the people in the story.

## Game Over

Characters → Jan asks Max to play.

Max runs out with his toy.

"What a throw!" Jan says.

"Oh no!" says Max.

"The toy is on the roof!"

**TURN and TALK** Talk about what makes the characters in "Game Over" seem real.

# Realistic Fiction Anchor Chart

**Characters**

"Let's play!"

**Setting**

**Events that seem real**

# The Blackout

## Preview Vocabulary

You will read these words in *The Blackout*.

| check | quiet | listen | mutters |
|-------|-------|--------|---------|

## Read

**Read** to learn about the characters.

**Look** at the pictures to help you understand what is happening in the story.

**Ask** about what the characters do.

**Talk** about the story with a partner.

### Meet *the* Author

**Zetta Elliott** used to be afraid of the dark. She still keeps lots of candles and batteries at home, just in case there is a blackout near her home.

Read Together | Genre | Realistic Fiction

AUDIO

Audio with Highlighting

ANNOTATE

# The Blackout

written by Zetta Elliott • illustrated by Maxime Lebrun

27

The lights went out
during the storm.

Everything went quiet.

"I will check on Mr. Stevens,"
Mama says.

"I will check on Martha and Todd," Papa says.

"I will check on Mrs. Johnson,"
I say.

CLOSE READ

Underline the words that tell
what the boy says.

I go upstairs with my flashlight.

Mrs. Johnson's radio was always on.

But now it is silent.

**VOCABULARY IN CONTEXT**

Underline the words that help you
figure out what **silent** means.

"I need a battery,"
Mrs. Johnson mutters.

I give her my battery.

CLOSE READ

How would you describe the boy?
Highlight the details that help you.

Mrs. Johnson puts my battery
in her radio.

It works!

Everyone comes.

We all listen until the lights come back on.

# Develop Vocabulary

 **MY TURN** <u>Underline</u> the word that completes each sentence.

1. We (<u>check</u> / mutters) on our friends when the lights go out.

2. The room is too (quiet / listen).

3. Mrs. Johnson (check / mutters) in the dark.

4. We (quiet / listen) to the radio together.

# Check for Understanding

**MY TURN** Write the answers to the questions. You can look back at the text.

**1.** How do you know this text is realistic fiction?

_____

- - - - - - - - - - - - - - - - - - - - - - - -

_____

- - - - - - - - - - - - - - - - - - - - - - - -

_____

**2.** How does the author describe the characters?

_____

- - - - - - - - - - - - - - - - - - - - - - - -

_____

- - - - - - - - - - - - - - - - - - - - - - - -

_____

**3.** How can you describe Mrs. Johnson? Use text evidence.

_____

- - - - - - - - - - - - - - - - - - - - - - - -

_____

- - - - - - - - - - - - - - - - - - - - - - - -

_____

# Describe a Character

A **character** is a person or animal in a story. When we describe a character, we tell what he or she looks like. We tell what the character says or does. Like real people, characters do things for a reason.

 **MY TURN** Describe the main character. Look back at the text. Use the pictures too.

**Character**

**What He Says**

_____
- - - - - - - - - - - - - - - - - - -
_____

_____
- - - - - - - - - - - - - - - - - - -
_____

**What He Does**

_____
- - - - - - - - - - - - - - - - - - -
_____

_____
- - - - - - - - - - - - - - - - - - -
_____

**TURN and TALK** Describe the reason the boy goes upstairs.

# Use Text Evidence

Text evidence is the details that support an idea about the text. Text evidence helps readers describe characters and the reasons for their actions.

**MY TURN** Draw the main character of *The Blackout.* Look back at the text.

# Reflect and Share

## Talk About It

Retell what happens in *The Blackout*. What are other ways to help neighbors that you have read about?

## Retell a Text

When retelling a text, it is important to:

- Tell about the events in your own words.
- Maintain, or keep, the same meaning as the text.

Use the words on the note to help you.

What do you mean?

Now retell the text.

**Weekly Question**

**How can neighbors help each other?**

I can make and use words to read and write realistic fiction.

My Learning Goal

# Academic Vocabulary

Related words can have the same word part.

**MY TURN** Write each word from the box with its related word.

| type | group | settle | various |
| --- | --- | --- | --- |

| **settled** | **grouped** |
| --- | --- |
| settle | |
| **typical** | **variety** |

43

**Read Together**

# Read Like a Writer, Write for a Reader

A **first-person text** is a story told by a character in the story. First-person texts use words such as **I**, **me**, **my**, and **we**.

> I go upstairs with my flashlight.

◄ · · · · · · · · The author uses these words to help readers understand that the story is a first-person text.

 **TURN and TALK** What do you picture in your mind when you think about the first-person text *The Blackout?*

**MY TURN** Write a sentence about something that happened to you. Use a word that shows it is a first-person text.

_____

-  -  -  -  -  -  -  -  -  -  -  -  -  -  -  -  -  -  -

_____

_____

-  -  -  -  -  -  -  -  -  -  -  -  -  -  -  -  -  -  -

_____

_____

-  -  -  -  -  -  -  -  -  -  -  -  -  -  -  -  -  -  -

_____

# Spell Short a Words

The short **a** sound is often spelled **a**.

 Read and spell the words.

| Spelling Words | | | |
|---|---|---|---|
| am | at | mat | sat |

**Short a**

am

**My Words to Know**

I     see

# Nouns

A **noun** names a person, animal, or thing.

Our **neighbor** brings his **cat** and a **flashlight**.

      ↑               ↑             ↑

(person)        (animal)      (thing)

**MY TURN** Edit the sentences by writing the best noun from the box.

| radio | boy | dog |
|-------|-----|-----|

1. The _____boy_____ can help.

2. He grabs a _____ .

3. He helps the _____ .

I can write a story.

## Meet the Author

An **author** is the person who writes a book.

**MY TURN** Read about the author. Underline the author's name. Highlight the information that tells about the author.

Wes has been writing since he was a kid. He likes to write about animals.

**TURN and TALK** Talk with a partner about what authors do.

# What Good Writers Do

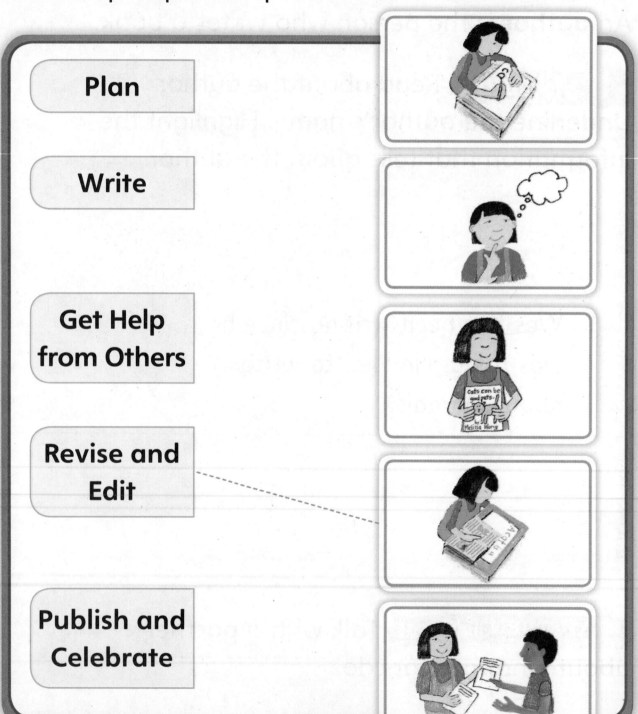

**MY TURN** Draw a line from each Writing Workshop step to the picture that shows what to do.

Plan

Write

Get Help from Others

Revise and Edit

Publish and Celebrate

# Writing Club

Writing Club is a group that shares ideas about writing. Your Writing Club will help you be a better writer.

## Writing Club Expectations

Do . . .

- relate, or tell, about your experience writing.
- express your needs and feelings about writing.

Don't . . .

- be shy. Teamwork leads to great results!
- make unhelpful comments.

**MY TURN** Introduce yourself to your Writing Club. Tell about what you like to write about.

# What Is in a Neighborhood?

 MY TURN Underline the name of each neighborhood place.

## Houses

A family can live here.

## Apartment

Lots of people can live here.

# What can I see in a neighborhood?

## Store

People can buy
food here.

## Park

Kids can play here.

# Middle Sounds

 **SEE and SAY** Say each picture name. Listen to the middle sound as you name each picture.

## Short i

Short **i** is often spelled **i**, as in **pin**.

**MY TURN** Read these words.

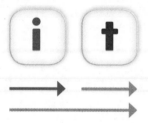

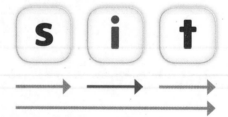

# Short i

 **TURN and TALK** Read these sentences with a partner.

 **Tim can sit.**

 **Can Tim sit?**

**MY TURN** Say each picture name. Write the letter **i** to finish the word. Say the picture name again.

 T___m

s___t

 ___p n

 ___s p

# Short i

**MY TURN** Write the letter **i** to finish the words. Read the sentence.

T___m can ___s t .

Say the sound for each letter. Then blend the sounds to read the words.

**MY TURN** Write a sentence about Tim.

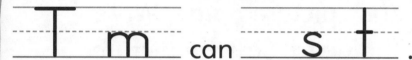

Tim

# Alliteration

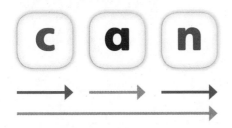 **SEE and SAY** Sometimes groups of words begin with the same initial sound. Say the picture names. Tell the sound that is the same in each picture name.

## Cc, Pp, Nn

The letter **c** makes the **k** sound in **cat**.
The letter **p** makes the **p** sound in **pin**.
The letter **n** makes the **n** sound in **nap**.

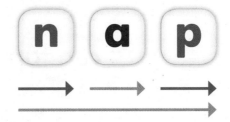 **MY TURN** Read each word.

c  a  n            n  a  p

# My Words to Know

Some words you must remember and practice.

**MY TURN** Read these words.

| we | do | the | one | like |
|----|----|----|----|----|

**MY TURN** Complete the sentences with words from the box. Read the sentences.

1. I _____like_____ the pan.

2. I tap _____ .

3. _____ we tap _____ pan?

4. _____ can tap and tap.

# Cc, Pp, Nn

**TURN and TALK** Read these words with a partner.

| | | |
|---|---|---|
| **can** | **pan** | **man** |
| **it** | **pit** | **sit** |
| **in** | **pin** | **tin** |
| **map** | **tap** | **cap** |

**MY TURN** Write **c**, **p**, or **n** to finish the words.

1. We ___p a t___ the ___a t___.

2. The cat can ___a p___.

**TURN and TALK** Read the sentences.

# Cc, Pp, Nn

 **MY TURN** Say each picture name. Write **c**, **p**, or **n** to complete the words. Then read the words.

m a p

__ a n

p i __

__ a t

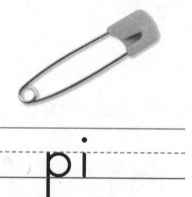 **MY TURN** Write a sentence about one of the pictures.

# Tip the Cat

We can see one cat.

We can see one pan.

Read the story. Highlight the four words with the **k** sound spelled **c.**

We can pat <u>Tip</u> the cat.

Tip can sit in the pan.

<u>Underline</u> the four words with the short **i** sound.

Tip can nap in the pan.

Do we like it?

We do!

Highlight the four words with the **n** sound.

**My Learning Goal**

I can read realistic fiction.

SPOTLIGHT ON GENRE

# Realistic Fiction

Realistic fiction has a setting.
The setting is when and where a story
happens. It can be real or seem real.

**Be a Fluent Reader** Fluent readers read
realistic fiction aloud with expression. After
you read this week's story, practice reading
fluently with a partner.

# Realistic Fiction: Anchor Chart

The setting is where and when a story takes place.

**In realistic fiction:**
the places are real or seem real

Dallas

farm

a school

the time is real or seems real

morning

at night

# from Henry on Wheels

## Preview Vocabulary

You will read these words in *Henry on Wheels.*

| sand | block | street | corner |
|------|-------|--------|--------|

## Read

> **Read** to enjoy the story.
>
> **Look** at the illustrations to help you understand what is happening.
>
> **Ask** questions about the setting.
>
> **Talk** about this story with a partner.

### Meet the Author

**Brian Biggs** created the *Everything Goes* series. He loves things that go. B.B. Bourne wrote this text in the style of Brian Biggs.

# from Everything Goes:
# Henry on Wheels
## by B.B. Bourne

AUDIO
Audio with Highlighting

ANNOTATE

illustrated by
Simon Abbott

65

Henry has a red bike.

Henry loves to ride his bike.

He can ride up and down.

Henry can ride by himself.

"I can ride far," Henry says.

"I want to take a long ride."

**VOCABULARY IN CONTEXT**

<u>Underline</u> the word that helps you figure out what **far** means.

"You may go," says Henry's mom.
"You may go around the block."

"Boring!" says Henry.

"But I will stay on our block."

Henry waves to his mom.

Then he rides away.

CLOSE READ

<u>Underline</u> the words that tell where Henry will ride.

Henry rides down the street.

He rides by a boy on a trike.

He rides by a girl skipping rope.

Henry rides past a cat.

He rides past two dogs.

Henry turns the corner.

He sees a line of people.

Henry stops to look.

"Wow!" says Henry.

Henry rides some more.

He sees a man with a shovel.

He sees a mixer too.

CLOSE READ

Highlight something in the text you have
a question about. To better understand,
ask yourself a question about it.

Henry stops to watch.

The barrel turns.

Gravel pours out.

Henry waves good-bye.

He rides around a corner.

Some big kids ride up.

"Nice bike," one kid says.

"Way to ride!" they say.

Henry rides down the street.

Henry sees kids swinging.

**CLOSE READ**

<u>Underline</u> the words on this page that tell where Henry rides his bike.

Henry sees kids sliding and playing in the sand.

Henry rides past.

He waves but does not stop.

Henry hears some noise.

He looks up the street.

"More machines!" he says.

CLOSE READ

Highlight something on page 78 that
you have a question about.

Henry stops to watch.

A bulldozer pushes dirt.

A dump truck backs up.

# A backhoe digs.

The dump truck drives away.

"Wow!" says Henry.

Henry watches a crane.

The crane swings around.

Men unhook the load.

The dump truck comes back.

The backhoe fills it up.

"What a good day," says Henry.

**FLUENCY**

Read pages 68 and 69 aloud with a partner to practice reading with expression.

# Develop Vocabulary

 **MY TURN** Use the words from the box to finish the sentences about the places Henry rides.

| sand | block | street | corner |
|------|-------|--------|--------|

Henry can ride around the ___block___ .

He rides his bike down the _____ .

At the _____ there is a line of people.

Henry sees kids playing in the _____ .

# Check for Understanding

**MY TURN** Write the answers to the questions. You can look back at the text.

**1.** What makes the setting realistic?

_____

_____

_____

_____

**2.** Why does the author keep Henry on his block?

_____

_____

_____

_____

**3.** How is your neighborhood like Henry's neighborhood? Use text evidence.

_____

_____

_____

_____

# Describe the Setting

The **setting** is where and when a story takes place.

**MY TURN** What is the setting of *Henry on Wheels?* Look back at the text.

The setting of *Henry on Wheels* is

_____

_____

_____

What details in the story help you describe the setting?

_____

_____

_____

# Ask and Answer Questions

Asking and answering questions about the setting as you read helps you better understand the text.

**MY TURN** Draw the answer to one of your questions about *Henry on Wheels*. Look back at the text.

**TURN and TALK** What questions do you have after reading the text?

**Read Together**

# Reflect and Share

**Write to Sources**

You read about Henry's neighborhood. On a separate sheet of paper, write about another realistic fiction story you have read. Use text evidence to show how the settings are similar or different.

## Use Text Evidence

When writing about texts, it is important to use text evidence, or examples from the text. You should:

• Find text evidence that supports your ideas.

**Weekly Question**

**What can I see in a neighborhood?**

Read
Together

I can make and use words to read
and write realistic fiction.

My
Learning
Goal

# Academic Vocabulary

**Synonyms** are words that have similar meanings.

 **MY TURN** Read each sentence.
Write a word from the box that can replace
the underlined word.

| type | group | various |
|------|-------|---------|

1. She needs a certain <u>kind</u> of fruit.

2. Our neighborhood has <u>different</u> places to

   _____

   have fun. _____

3. The <u>crowd</u> meets at the park. _____

# Read Like a Writer, Write for a Reader

Authors choose words to help readers understand how characters feel about what they see.

> Henry stops to look. "Wow!" says Henry.

The author uses this word to express how Henry feels about seeing the trucks.

**MY TURN** Write some words or phrases that show how you would express your feelings about seeing something new.

_____

- - - - - - - - - - - - - - - - - - - -

_____

- - - - - - - - - - - - - - - - - - - -

_____

- - - - - - - - - - - - - - - - - - - -

_____

- - - - - - - - - - - - - - - - - - - -

# Spell Short i Words

Some words follow a spelling pattern. The short **i** sound is often spelled **i**, as in **pin.** Other words do not follow a pattern. You must remember how to spell them.

**MY TURN** Read and spell the short **i** words. Then spell the My Words to Know words.

## Spelling Words

| it | sit | mitt | miss |

### Short i

### My Words to Know

| the | one |

# Present Verb Tense

A **verb** is an action word. **Present verb tense** tells about action that is happening now.

Henry **sees** Max. (present verb tense)

They **ride** on the block. (present verb tense)

**MY TURN** Edit the sentences by writing a present tense verb from the box.

| jump | walks | plays |
|------|-------|-------|

1. Henry ~~walks~~ to the park.

   _____

2. He _____ with his dad.

   _____

3. They _____ .

I can write a story.

# Where Authors Get Ideas

Authors get their ideas from their experiences or their imaginations. They get ideas by looking around too.

**MY TURN** What do you want to write about? Use the chart to draw or write your ideas.

| Ideas | Where Did the Idea Come From? |
|---|---|
|  |  |
|  |  |
|  |  |

# Digital Tools We Can Use

Computers and tablets are types of **digital tools.** We can use digital tools to help us write.

**MY TURN** Look at the two styles of writing. Highlight the difference in the two types of writing.

The big cat can sit. He will take a nap.

The BIG cat can sit. He will take a nap.

**TURN and TALK** Talk with a partner about how digital tools can make you a better writer.

# Digital Tools We Can Use Together

Authors use digital tools to find information to use in their writing. They work with others to write with digital tools.

 **MY TURN** Read the list of rules for using digital tools. Check each box when you use digital tools.

- ☐ Ask before you use any digital tool.

- ☐ Only go to websites approved by your teacher.

- ☐ Ask for help to find pictures for your writing.

- ☐ Share the digital tool with others.

**Read Together**

# Traffic Signals

 **MY TURN** <u>Underline</u> the names of the traffic signals that help keep you safe.

## Traffic Light

A traffic light lets people know when it is safe to cross the street.

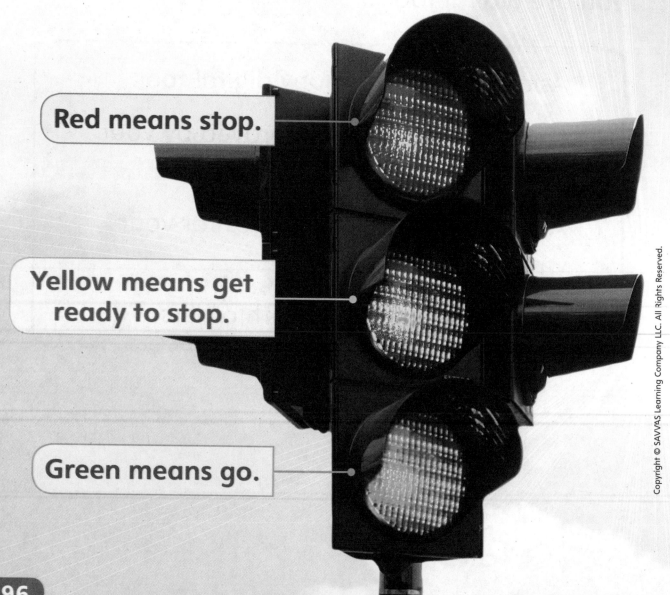

Red means stop.

Yellow means get ready to stop.

Green means go.

## How do signs in our neighborhood help us?

# Walk and Wait Signals

Walk and wait signals let people know when it is safe to cross the street.

Cross

Do not cross

# Middle Sounds

 **SEE and SAY** Say the sounds as you name each picture. Listen to the middle vowel sound. Then say the name of each picture again.

## Short o

Short **o** is often spelled **o**, as in **top**.

**MY TURN** Read these words.

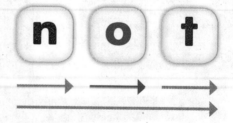

# Short o

 **TURN** and **TALK** Read these words with a partner.

| | | |
|---|---|---|
|  | **on** | **not** |
| 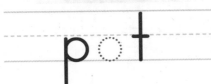 | **Tom** | **mom** |

 **MY TURN** Say each picture name. Write the letter **o** to finish the word. Then read the words.

p o t

m    p

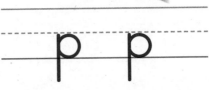

t    p

p    p

## Short o

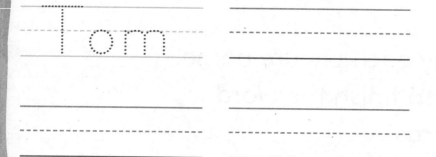 **MY TURN** Read the sentence. <u>Underline</u> the short **o** words. Then write the words on the lines.

Tom can see the pot on top.

Tom

Listen for the short **o** sound that you hear in **mop**.

**MY TURN** Draw a picture to show the sentence about Tom. Label the picture with a short **o** word.

# Alliteration

 **SEE and SAY** Sometimes words begin with the same onset, or beginning, sound. Say the picture names. Tell the onset sound of each picture name.

## Ff, Bb, Gg

The letter **f** makes the **f** sound in **fan**.
The letter **b** makes the **b** sound in **bat**.
The letter **g** makes the **g** sound in **got**.

**MY TURN** Read these words.

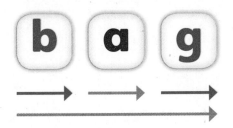 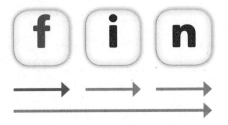

# My Words to Know

Some words you must remember and practice.

**MY TURN** Read these words.

| by | are | was | you | look |
|----|-----|-----|-----|------|

**MY TURN** Complete the sentences with words from the box. Read the sentences.
**Handwriting** Print the words clearly.

1. Look at the pig!

2. It _____ _____ the bin.

3. I see a pig by _____ .

4. We _____ by the bin.

# Ff, Bb, Gg

**TURN and TALK** Decode these words with a partner.

| | | | |
|---|---|---|---|
| | big | fig | pig |
| | got | pot | not |
| | tin | fin | pin |
| | sit | bit | fit |

**MY TURN** Write **f**, **b**, or **g** to finish the words.

1. Can the ___pig_____ ___it___ ?

2. The pig is ___ig___ .

**TURN and TALK** Read the sentences.

# Ff, Bb, Gg

**MY TURN** Draw a line from each word to the picture it names. Then write the words.

bib — bib

fan

gas

**MY TURN** Choose one word you wrote. Write a sentence with that word.

# Big Biff

Mom was by the bin.
Biff was not.
Look at Biff, Mom!

OPEN

AUDIO

Audio with Highlighting

ANNOTATE

Read the story. Underline the six words that have the **b** sound.

Biff got on top.

You are big, Biff

You do not fit on top.

**Highlight** the two words that have the **g** sound.

# Do not sit on top!

**Highlight** the three words with the short **o** sound.

**My Learning Goal** I can read about a neighborhood.

## Informational Text

An informational text tells facts about real people, things, or events. It may have text features, such as headings.

### Neighborhoods

**Heading** **PLACES**

There are many places in a neighborhood. There is a market where people buy food. There is a school where children learn.

**TURN and TALK** What makes informational text different from realistic fiction?

Informational Text
Anchor Chart

# PLACES IN THE NEIGHBORHOOD

Fact

Heading ↵
"what a section is about"
"helps you find information"

Fact

# Look Both Ways!

## Preview Vocabulary

You will read these words in *Look Both Ways!*

| left | right | guard | crosswalk |
|------|-------|-------|-----------|

## Read

**Read** to learn about being safe when crossing the street.

**Look** at the pictures and headings.

**Ask** questions about information you do not understand.

**Talk** about the most important ideas.

### Meet the Author

**Janet Klausner** grew up in a big city, where streets were busy with traffic day and night. She has never forgotten how important it is to "look both ways" before crossing the street.

# LOOK BOTH WAYS!

written by Janet Klausner

 AUDIO

Audio with Highlighting

 ANNOTATE

**Crosswalk**

# Lines

What do these lines in the street tell you?

Lines show a safe place to cross.

First, look both ways!

**CLOSE READ**

Underline the label that helps you find the crosswalk in the picture.

# Crossing Guards

What does this guard tell you?

Walk when this guard tells you it is safe.

First, look both ways!

**CLOSE READ**

Why does the author use the heading **Crossing Guards?** Highlight the details that help you tell why.

# Pictures

What do these two pictures tell you?

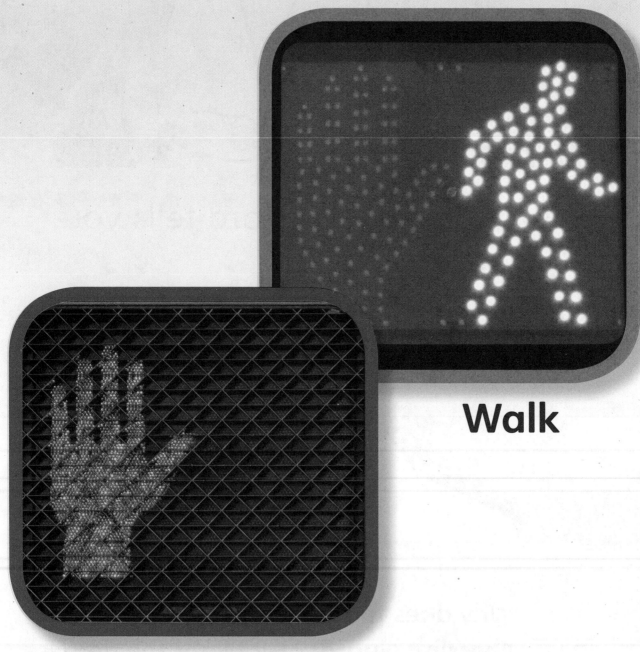

**Walk**

**Wait**

Walk when the picture shows a person.

First, look both ways!

CLOSE READ

Underline the heading that tells what these pages are all about.

# Safety

Look at all the traffic!

How will you walk safely?

Traffic

Look left, look right,
look left again.

Then walk safely!

# Glossary

crosswalk

traffic

**VOCABULARY IN CONTEXT**

What does the word **traffic** mean? How does the picture help you figure it out?

# Develop Vocabulary

**MY TURN** Draw a line from each word to the picture that shows its meaning.

left

right

guard

crosswalk

# Check for Understanding

**MY TURN** Write the answers to the questions. You can look back at the text.

**1.** How do you know this is an informational text?

_____

_____

_____

_____

**2.** Why does the author use the title *Look Both Ways!* for this text?

_____

_____

_____

_____

**3.** Why should you look both ways before you cross the street? Use text evidence.

_____

_____

_____

_____

# Find Text Features

Text features help you find and learn information.
A **heading** tells the topic of a section.
A **label** names what a picture shows.

**MY TURN** What can you learn from the
text features in *Look Both Ways!?* Look back
at the text.

| Text Feature | What I Learned |
|---|---|
| Label | |
| Heading | |

# Use Text Evidence

Text evidence is the details that support what a reader thinks about the text and text features.

**MY TURN** Draw the details that support the heading **Crossing Guards.** Look back at the text. Use the pictures too.

# Reflect and Share

## Talk About It

Retell *Look Both Ways!* in your own words. How is this text similar to other texts you have read about neighborhoods?

## Listening to Others

When sharing ideas with others, it is important to:

- Be quiet when others are speaking.

- Face the speaker to show you are listening.

Look at the picture to help you.

**Weekly Question**

**How do signs in our neighborhood help us?**

**Read Together**

My Learning Goal

I can make and use words to connect reading and writing.

# Academic Vocabulary

**Context clues** help you understand what an unknown word means. The clues can be words around the unknown word.

**MY TURN** Read each sentence. Highlight the context clue for the underlined word.

1. This is a new <u>group</u>, or set, of books.

2. We will live here and <u>settle</u> in this neighborhood.

3. The <u>various</u> homes look different from each other.

# Read Like a Writer, Write for a Reader

Authors use print features such as headings to help readers find information.

**Crossing Guards** ◀······
What does this guard tell you?

The author puts information into sections with headings to help readers find information they need.

**TURN** *and* **TALK** Find a print feature in the text. Discuss why the author uses that feature.

**MY TURN** Write a sentence about crossing the street. Then write a heading that tells what the sentence is about.

**Heading:** _____

_____

_____

_____

# Spell Short o Words

The short **o** sound is often spelled **o**.
When we alphabetize a series, or list, of words,
we write them in order of the alphabet.

**MY TURN** Alphabetize the words in each set
to the first letter.

| Spelling Words | | | |
| --- | --- | --- | --- |
| not | got | cot | pot |

cot

| My Words to Know |
| --- |
| look     you |

# Simple Sentences

A **simple sentence** tells a complete idea. It has a subject and verb. The **subject** is the naming part. The **verb** is the action part. A sentence begins with a capital letter and ends with a punctuation mark.

The girl walks. (complete idea)

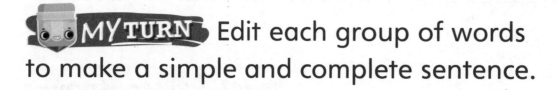 **MY TURN** Edit each group of words to make a simple and complete sentence.

**1.** cars the stop

_____

\_ \_ \_ \_ \_ \_ \_ \_ \_ \_ \_ \_ \_ \_ \_ \_ \_ \_ \_ \_ \_ \_ \_ \_ \_ \_ \_ \_

_____

**2.** helps guard the

_____

\_ \_ \_ \_ \_ \_ \_ \_ \_ \_ \_ \_ \_ \_ \_ \_ \_ \_ \_ \_ \_ \_ \_ \_ \_ \_ \_ \_

_____

**My Learning Goal**

I can write a story.

# Features of a Fiction Book

The **front cover** tells the title and the names of the author and illustrator.

The **back cover** tells details about the book.

The **title page** is near the front of the book. It tells the title, the author, and publisher of a book.

**MY TURN** (Circle) the book part that provides each piece of information.

| illustrator's name | front cover | back cover |
|---|---|---|
| book title | back cover | title page |
| details | back cover | front cover |
| author's name | title page | front cover |

# Features of a Nonfiction Book

A **table of contents** tells the section titles in a book.

An **index** is a list of the topics in a book and the pages that have information about each topic.

A **glossary** is at the back of a book. It tells the meanings of important words in the book.

**MY TURN** (Circle) the part of a book that tells the meanings of important words.

**Highlight** the part of a book that tells the section titles.

Underline the part of a book that lists the topics.

| Table of Contents | |
| --- | --- |
| Crossing the Street | 2 |
| Traffic Signals | 5 |

| Index |
| --- |
| **Safety** 2, 3, 15 |
| **Stop sign** 8, 9, 12–13 |

| Glossary |
| --- |
| **crosswalk** area marked with lines that people use to cross the street |
| **stop light** traffic light |

# Making and Responding to Suggestions

An important part of writing is talking with others about ways to make your writing better. You can suggest ways others can make their writing better too.

**MY TURN** Highlight two ways to make suggestions to others about their writing.

I think this part needs a picture.

I like the characters and what they do.

Could you tell more about this character?

**TURN and TALK** Talk with a partner about how you can respond to the suggestions above.

# Neighborhood Activities

## Block Party!
Neighbors get together to have fun, eat food, play games, and listen to music.

## Yard Sale!
Yard sales help neighbors sell the stuff they don't need.

## How can I get to know my neighbors?

**Plant a Tree!**
Neighbors can work together
to plant a new tree.

**TURN and TALK** What activities
does your neighborhood have?

# Middle Sounds

 **SEE and SAY** Say each picture name. Listen to the middle sound as you name each picture.

## Short e

Short **e** is often spelled **e**, as in **pen**.

**MY TURN** Read each word.

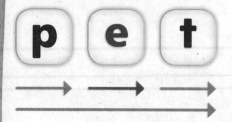 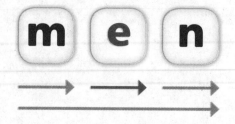

# Short e

 **TURN and TALK** Read these words with a partner.

| | | |
|---|---|---|
| **set** | **get** | **met** |

| | | |
|---|---|---|
| **men** | **pen** | **Ben** |

 **MY TURN** Say each picture name. Write **e** to finish each word. Then read the words.

m e n

p t

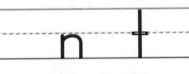

n t

t n

Read
Together

# Short e

**MY TURN** Read the sentences. <u>Underline</u> words with the short **e** sound.

Peg the cat met ten men.

One man was Ben.

Peg sat by Ben.

Ben did pet Peg.

Listen for the short **e** sound you hear in **set**.

**MY TURN** Write another sentence about Peg and Ben.

Peg and Ben

# Initial Sounds

 Say each picture name.
Listen to the beginning sound as you name
each picture.

## Dd, Ll, Hh

The letter **d** makes the **d** sound in **dig**.
The letter **l** makes the **l** sound in **leg**.
The letter **h** makes the **h** sound in **hat**.

 Read each word.

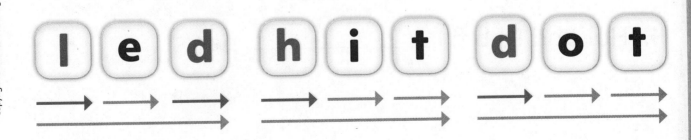

# My Words to Know

Some words you must remember and practice.

**MY TURN** Read the words.

| up | two | that | have | they |
|----|-----|------|------|------|

**MY TURN** Write words from the box to complete the sentences. Read the sentences.

1. They are _____ the hill.

2. Hal and Deb _____ to dig.

3. The _____ dig in the hill.

4. Hal and Deb fill _____ pen.

# Dd, Ll, Hh

**TURN and TALK** Read these words with a partner.

| bed | let | hen |
|-----|-----|-----|
| dig | lip | him |

**MY TURN** Write **d**, **l**, or **h** to finish the words.

1. Sam can see the ___ h e n ___ .

2. It is in the ___ b e ___ .

3. Sam ___ e t ___ it nap.

**TURN and TALK** Now read the sentences.

# Dd, Ll, Hh

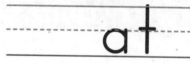 **MY TURN** Say each picture name. Write **d**, **l**, or **h** to finish each picture name.

\_\_\_\_ eg          \_\_\_\_ be          \_\_\_\_ at

**MY TURN** Write a sentence that includes a word with **d**, **l**, or **h**.

_____

_____

_____

# Fill the Pen

Hal can dig in the hill.

Deb can dig.

Two can dig a lot.

Read the story. Highlight the four words with the **I** sound.

<u>Hal</u> let Deb dig in the hill.

They have a BIG pen.

They can fill it up.

<u>Underline</u> the three words with the **h** sound.

Highlight the two words with the **d** sound.

They get hot.

Look at that pen!

They did it!

Highlight the two words with the short **e** sound.

**My Learning Goal**

I can read realistic fiction.

**SPOTLIGHT ON GENRE**

# Realistic Fiction

Characters are the people in realistic fiction. Details describe characters and the reasons for their actions.

**TURN and TALK** Describe the reason the boy helps Mrs. Johnson in *The Blackout*.

**Set a Purpose** It is important to think about why you are reading. Your purpose, or reason, could be to learn or to have fun.

# Realistic Fiction Anchor Chart

## character
> Pam

### Character Details

words ⟷ & ⟷ pictures

Pam jumps up and down. "YES!" Pam said.

tell more about the character
> Pam is happy!

# Garden Party

## Preview Vocabulary

You will read these words in *Garden Party*.

| plant | help |
|-------|------|

## Read and Compare

**Think** about why you will read this text.

**Read** for the purpose you set.

**Look** for words and pictures to help you understand the characters.

**Ask** questions about the characters.

**Compare** this text to *Click, Clack, Click!*

### Meet the Author

**Charles R. Smith Jr.** is an author, photographer, and poet. He has written more than 30 books. Charles is especially proud that many kids who don't like to read do like to read his books.

# Garden Party

AUDIO

Audio with Highlighting

ANNOTATE

written by Charles R. Smith Jr.    illustrated by Debbie Palen

COMMUNITY GARDEN

"We got the spot for our garden!" said Dad.

"How can we plant the garden?" asked Jamal. "It's so big."

"We can have a garden party," said Mom.

"Right," said Dad. "Our neighbors will help."

"They will?" asked Jamal.

**VOCABULARY IN CONTEXT**

What does the word **garden** mean? What part of the pictures help you figure it out?

First, they went to the tall
apartment building on State
Street. "We will help," their
neighbors said.

Next, they went to the red brick houses near the park. "We will help," their neighbors said.

**CLOSE READ**

What can you understand about the neighbors? Highlight the details that help you.

151

Last, they went to all the little stores on Main Street. "We will help," their neighbors said.

"You were right, Dad," said Jamal. "Our neighbors did help!"

"That's what neighbors do," said Dad.

**CLOSE READ**

How does Jamal feel now? Underline the text that helps you describe Jamal.

# Click, Clack, Click!

## Preview Vocabulary

You will read these words in *Click, Clack, Click!*

| meet | join |
|------|------|

## Read and Compare

**Think** about why you will read this text.

**Read** for the purpose you set.

**Look** for words and pictures to help you understand the characters.

**Ask** questions about the characters.

**Compare** this text to *Garden Party*.

### Meet the Author

**F. Isabel Campoy** loves music, dancing, and collecting musical instruments. She lived in Boston for 15 years. Now she lives in San Francisco.

# Click, Clack, Click!

written by F. Isabel Campoy

illustrated by Peter Francis

COMMUNITY CENTER

WELCOME

 AUDIO

Audio with Highlighting

 ANNOTATE

**155**

Amena just moved here. She doesn't know anyone. Amena and her mom walk to the center to meet friends.

"What are you playing?"
Amena asks.

"These are pieces of wood,"
Adnan says. "You clink them
together."

**CLOSE READ**

How do you think Amena feels?
Underline the text that helps you
describe Amena.

"What are you playing?"
Amena asks.

"It is a wooden box," Kim
says. "You beat on it."

"What are you playing?"
Amena asks.

"It is a gourd," Gabriel says.
"You move the beads."

"Do you want to join our neighborhood band?" they ask.

"I don't have an instrument to play," Amena says.

"Yes, you do!" they say.
"You have a jar."

Now Amena has an instrument.
And friends too!

**CLOSE READ**

How does Amena feel now?
Underline the text that helps
you describe Amena.

**Read Together**

# Develop Vocabulary

**MY TURN** Draw a line from each word to the word group where it best fits.

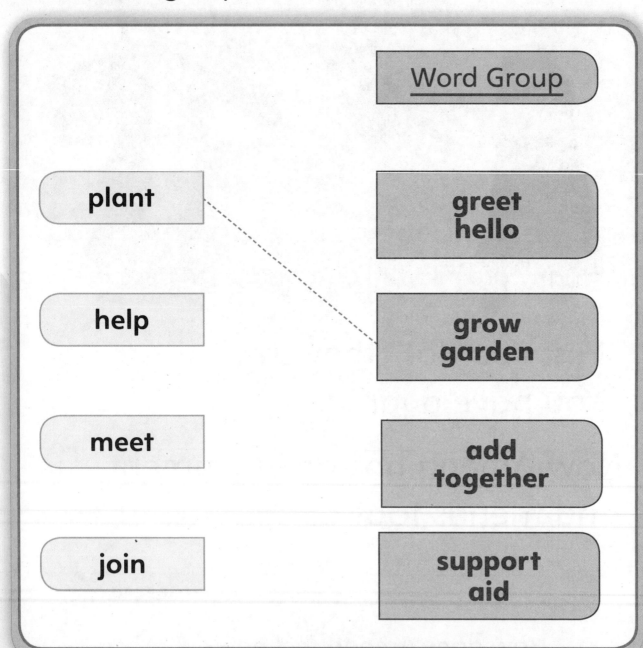

Word Group

| | |
|---|---|
| plant | greet hello |
| help | grow garden |
| meet | add together |
| join | support aid |

**Read Together**

# Check for Understanding

**MY TURN** Write the answers to the questions. You can look back at the texts.

1. What makes both texts realistic fiction?

_____

_____

_____

_____

2. What words do the authors use to describe things? Why do they use these words?

_____

_____

_____

_____

3. How are the texts alike? Use text evidence.

_____

_____

_____

_____

# Describe Characters

**Characters** are the people or animals in a story. To compare characters, describe how they are alike. To contrast characters, describe how they are different.

 **MY TURN** Draw to compare and contrast how Jamal and Amena act. Look back at the texts.

| Alike | Different |
|---|---|
| | |

# Visualize Details

The details in a story can help readers make pictures in their minds about the characters and events.

**MY TURN** How do you picture the neighbors in *Garden Party?* Draw the picture you see in your mind. Look back at the text.

# Reflect and Share

## Talk About It

You read about how Jamal and Amena get to know their neighbors. How would you get to know neighbors if you were Jamal or Amena?

## Make Connections

When describing personal connections to a text, think about:

- Your experiences.
- Feelings you have had.

This reminds me of . . .

Use the words on the note to help you.

Now share your connections.

**Weekly Question**

**How can I get to know my neighbors?**

I can make and use words to read and write realistic fiction.

## Academic Vocabulary

**Word parts** can be added to some words to make new words with different meanings.

**Re-** is a word part. It means **"again."**

**MY TURN** Write the meanings of the new words.

re- + group = regroup    to group again

re- + pack   = repack

re- + place  = replace

# Read Like a Writer, Write for a Reader

Authors choose words that can help readers visualize people, places, and events in a story.

Next, they went to the red brick **houses** near the park.

◄ • • • • • • •

The author chose these words to help readers picture what the houses look like.

 **MY TURN** Write sentences with words that tell what your school looks like.

_____

- - - - - - - - - - - - - - - - - - - - - - - - - - - -

_____

- - - - - - - - - - - - - - - - - - - - - - - - - - - -

_____

- - - - - - - - - - - - - - - - - - - - - - - - - - - -

_____

- - - - - - - - - - - - - - - - - - - - - - - - - - - -

_____

# Spell Short e Words

Short **e** is often spelled **e**, as in **bed**. When you write a series, or list, of words in the order of the alphabet, you alphabetize the words.

**MY TURN** Spell the words. Alphabetize the words in each set to the first letter.

### Spelling Words

| set | met | pet | net |
|-----|-----|-----|-----|

### Short e

met

### My Words to Know

have     they

# Adjectives and Articles

An **adjective** describes something.

See the **pretty** flowers.
(describes the flowers)

**A, an,** and **the** are articles, or determiners. **A** and **an** tell about any person, place, or thing. **The** tells about a specific person, place, or thing.

Flowers grow in **a** garden. (tells about any garden)

**MY TURN** Edit each sentence by adding an article and an adjective.

1. Tom gets ___an old___ flower pot.

2. He brings it to _____ garden.

3. Tom helps plant _____ tree.

My Learning Goal

I can write a story.

# Adding Details to Illustrations

Authors revise their drafts by adding details to illustrations. This makes their writing better. The details can tell more about what the words say.

 **MY TURN** Revise the illustration by adding details.

Rick is ready for school.

# Adding Details to Words

Authors add details to their words to make their writing better. They can use words such as **and, but, or, so**, and **because** to add details.

**MY TURN** Rewrite the sentences with added details.

**1.** My teacher is kind.

_____

----------------------------------------

_____

----------------------------------------

_____

----------------------------------------

_____

**2.** My classroom is fun.

_____

----------------------------------------

_____

_____

----------------------------------------

_____

# Asking and Answering Questions

Authors often meet to help make each other's writing better. They ask and answer questions about each other's writing.

**MY TURN** Read your partner's writing. Write a question about it.

_____

- - - - - - - - - - - - - - - - - - - - - - - - -

_____

_____

- - - - - - - - - - - - - - - - - - - - - - - - -

_____

_____

- - - - - - - - - - - - - - - - - - - - - - - - -

_____

_____

- - - - - - - - - - - - - - - - - - - - - - - - -

_____

**TURN and TALK** Have your partner read your writing. Answer your partner's question about it.

# Kinds of Neighborhoods

## Urban

An urban neighborhood is in a city. Many people live close together in an urban neighborhood.

## Suburban

A suburban neighborhood is near a city. People live farther apart in a suburban neighborhood.

## What does a neighborhood look like?

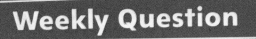 **TURN** and **TALK** What kind of neighborhood do you live in? Talk about it with a partner.

## Rural

A rural neighborhood is in the country. People live far apart in a rural neighborhood.

# Middle Sounds

 Say each sound as you name each picture. Listen to the middle sound. Tell the middle sound you hear in each picture name.

# Short u

Short **u** is often spelled **u**, as in **sun**.

 Read these words.

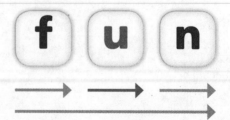

# Short u

 **TURN and TALK** Read these words with a partner.

| | | |
|---|---|---|
| **dug** | **hug** | **mug** |

| | | |
|---|---|---|
| **but** | **nut** | **hut** |

**MY TURN** Say each picture name.
Write the word on the lines. Read the words.

_____

_____

s u n

_____

_____

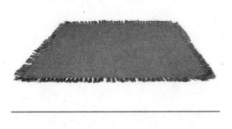

_____

_____

_____

_____

**Read Together**

# Short u

**MY TURN** Add **u** to make words. Read the words. Draw a line from each word to its picture.

| s | u | n |
|---|---|---|

| c |  | p |
|---|---|---|

| n |  | t |
|---|---|---|

| t |  | b |
|---|---|---|

**MY TURN** Write a sentence using words with short **u**.

_____

_____

_____

# Initial Sounds

**SEE and SAY** Say each sound as you name each picture. Listen to the sound at the beginning of each word.

## Rr, Ww, Jj, Kk

The letter **r** makes the **r** sound in **red**.
The letter **w** makes the **w** sound in **win**.
The letter **j** makes the **j** sound in **jet**.
The letter **k** makes the **k** sound in **kit**.

**MY TURN** Read these words.

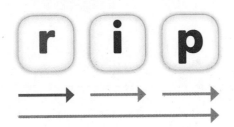

# My Words to Know

Some words you must remember and practice.

**MY TURN** Read the words.

| as | he | to | with | three |
|----|----|----|------|-------|

**MY TURN** Use words from the box to complete the sentences. Read the sentences.

1. Ken and Kim jog ___with___ Jim.

2. The _____ get hot in the sun.

3. Ken will run _____ the bus.

4. _____ is not _____ hot.

# Rr, Ww, Jj, Kk

**TURN and TALK** Decode these words with a partner.

| | | |
|---|---|---|
| **rag** | **rat** | **rug** |
| **web** | **wag** | **wet** |
| **jet** | **jug** | **Jan** |
| **Ken** | **kit** | **kid** |

**MY TURN** Write the letter **r**, **w**, **j**, or **k** to finish the words. Then read the sentences.

1. Kim will ___og.

2. Wes ___ill ___un.

3. Can ___im win?

# Rr, Ww, Jj, Kk

 **MY TURN** Write the word that completes each sentence.

rug

web

Think about which word makes sense in the sentence.

_____

1. We sit on the _____ .

_____

2. I see a big _____ .

 **MY TURN** Write a sentence that includes words with **r**, **w**, **j**, or **k**.

_____

_____

_____

_____

# Three Will Run

Ken will jog with Kim.

He will jog with Jeff.

The three like to run.

AUDIO

Audio with Highlighting

ANNOTATE

Read the story. <u>Underline</u> the three words with the **j** sound.
Highlight the two words that begin with the **k** sound spelled **k.**

They jog in the sun.

They will get red.

They jog in the mud.

They will get wet.

Highlight the three words with the
**w** sound.

But the three jog to the top.

They have fun as they jog.

<u>Underline</u> the two words with
the short **u** sound.

**My Learning Goal** I can read about a neighborhood.

## Procedural Text

A procedural text explains how to do or make something. It usually includes directions, or steps, to follow.

### From School to My House

**Steps in Order**

1. Go out the front door.

2. Turn right.

3. Walk three blocks.

**Verbs Tell What to Do**

4. Turn left.

5. Go to the red house.

**TURN and TALK** How is procedural text different from realistic fiction?

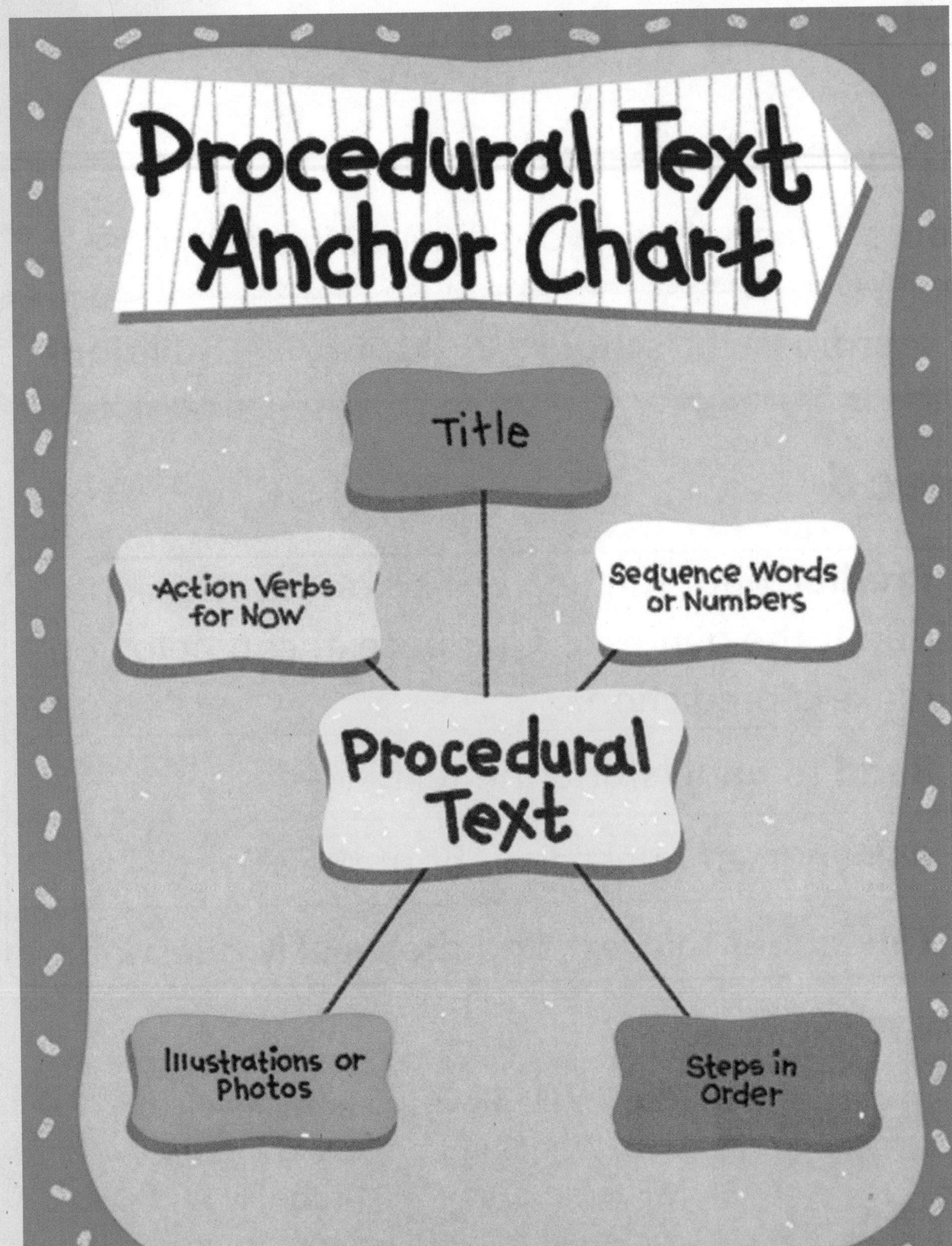

# Procedural Text Anchor Chart

Title

Action Verbs for NOW

Sequence Words or Numbers

## Procedural Text

Illustrations or Photos

Steps in Order

# Making a Map

## Preview Vocabulary

You will read these words in *Making a Map*.

| stores | school | library | buildings |

## Read

**Predict** what the text will be about. Thinking about the genre, or type of text, can help you make a prediction.

**Read** to understand the text.

**Ask** yourself questions about the steps.

**Talk** about this text and the weekly question.

### Meet *the* Author

**Gary Miller** loves to hike, kayak, and fish. When he's not exploring the wilderness, you will probably find him reading or playing his guitar.

# Making a Map

written by Gary Miller
illustrated by Valentina Belloni

**MY MAP**

Library

Green Street

Hillside Park

Main Street

My home

Elm Street

Elm Street School

Grocery Store

Oak Street

First Street

Buildings
Parks-Fields
Water

**Map Key**

Pet Store

Long Pond

AUDIO

Audio with Highlighting

ANNOTATE

Maps help people find their way.

Make a map of your neighborhood.

It will help others find places.

- Elm Street School
- Pet Store
- Grocery Store
- Library
- Hillside Park
- Long Pond

My Home

First, list some places you go.

CLOSE READ

What do you think you will learn about making a map? Highlight the words that help you. Use the pictures too.

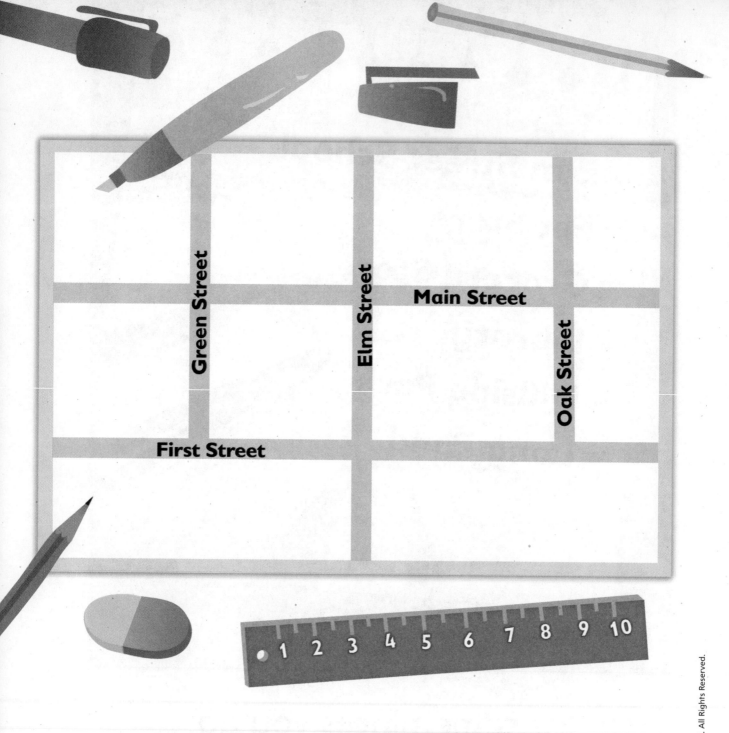

Then start your map.

Draw the streets near your home.

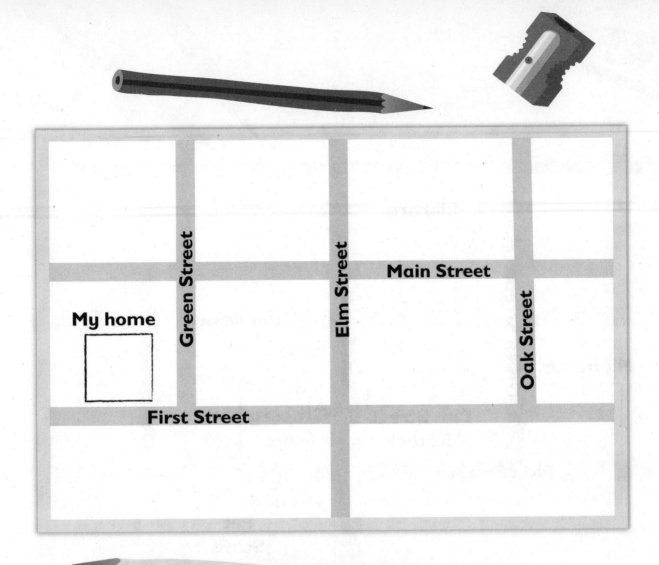

Add the places from your list.

Draw your home first.

Use squares to show buildings.

**CLOSE READ**

Look at the graphic, or map.
<u>Underline</u> the words in the text that
name what is on the map.

Library

Green Street

My home

Elm Street

Main Street

Elm Street School

Oak Street

Grocery Store

First Street

Pet Store

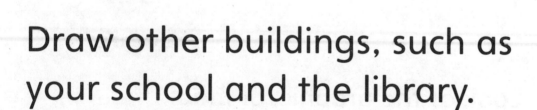

Draw other buildings, such as your school and the library.

Add stores too.

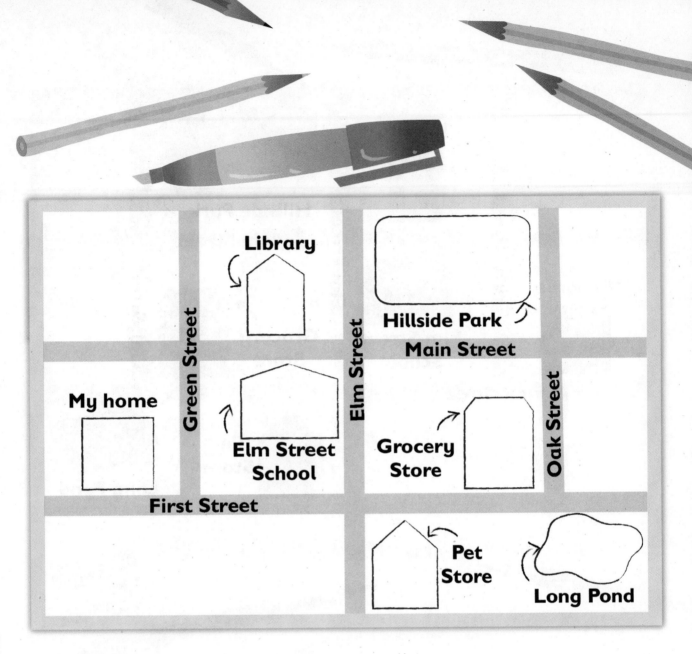

Add outdoor places, such as parks and ponds.

CLOSE READ

Look at the graphic, or map. <u>Underline</u> the words in the text that help you learn information about the map.

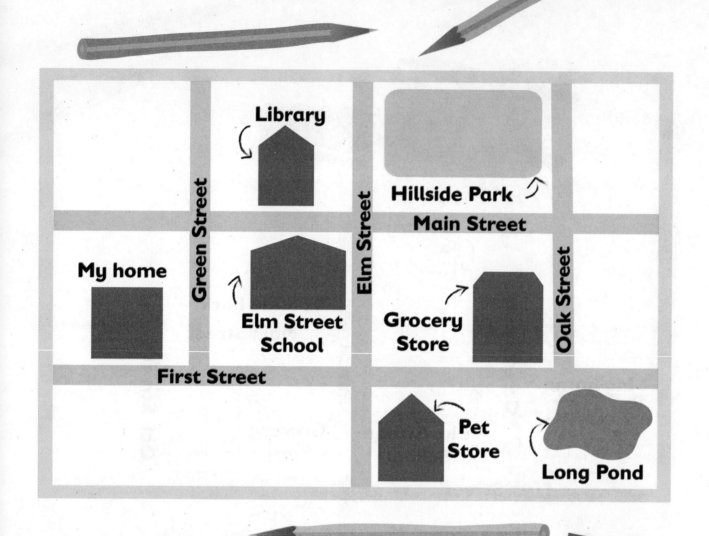

Next, color the places.

Use red for buildings.

Use green for parks and fields.

Use blue for water.

Last, make a key.

The key shows what the colors on the map mean.

Your map is ready to use!

**VOCABULARY IN CONTEXT**

Underline words that help you figure out what **fields** means. Use the picture too.

# Develop Vocabulary

**MY TURN** Write the word from the box that completes each sentence.

| stores | school | library | buildings |
|--------|--------|---------|-----------|

Look at my neighborhood map!

There are many buildings.

The _____ is where I get books.

I go to _____ to learn things.

My dad takes me to _____ to buy things.

**Read Together**

# Check for Understanding

**MY TURN** Write the answers to the questions. You can look back at the text.

**1.** What makes this text a procedural text?

_____

_____

_____

_____

**2.** Why do you think the author labels the pictures?

_____

_____

_____

_____

**3.** Why are there steps to making a map? Use text evidence.

_____

_____

_____

_____

# Find Graphics

Graphics, such as pictures, help readers find or learn information. The pictures in a text can give more information about the topic and important ideas.

**MY TURN** Write the word that names each part of the map. Look back at the text.

house

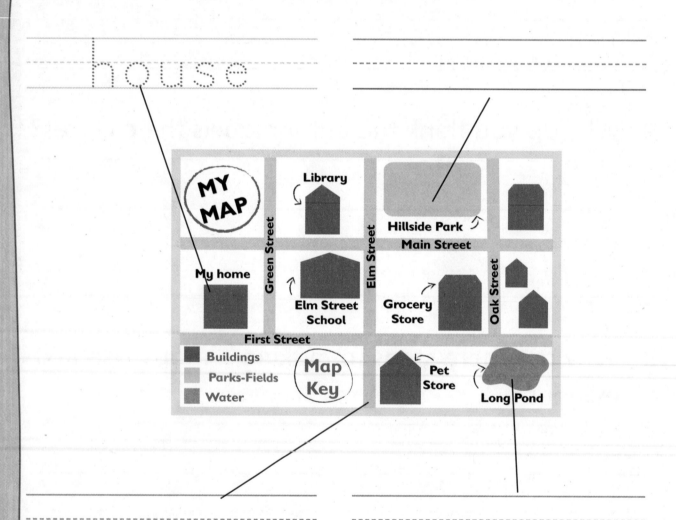

# Correct and Confirm Predictions

A **prediction** tells what you think will happen next. You can use text features to correct, or change, your prediction. After you read, you can confirm if your prediction was right.

**MY TURN** Think about your prediction. Look back at the text. Draw what made you change your prediction.

Was your prediction correct?          **Yes**     **No**

**Read Together**

# Reflect and Share

## Write to Sources

Think about the texts *Kinds of Neighborhoods* and *Making a Map*. On a separate sheet of paper, write brief comments about what you learned from each text. How are these informational texts alike? How are they different?

## Compare and Contrast

When writing about texts, you can compare and contrast the topics and information. You should:

- Use text evidence, or examples, from both texts.

- Explain how the examples are alike and different.

**Weekly Question**

**What does a neighborhood look like?**

I can make and use words to connect reading and writing.

**My Learning Goal**

# Academic Vocabulary

We practice new words when we use them in conversation.

**TURN and TALK** Use these sentences to talk with a partner about neighborhoods.

Describe different **types** of neighborhoods.

How can **groups** of people help neighborhoods?

Name the **various** places you can find in a neighborhood.

What makes a person want to **settle** in a neighborhood?

# Read Like a Writer, Write for a Reader

Authors choose words in a procedural text to help readers understand the steps.

> First, list some places you go. Next, color the places. Last, make a key.

The author uses these words to show the steps in order.

**MY TURN** Write sentences that tell how to make or do something. Use words that tell the steps in order.

_____

- - - - - - - - - - - - - - - - - - - - - - - - - - - - - -

_____

_____

- - - - - - - - - - - - - - - - - - - - - - - - - - - - - -

_____

_____

- - - - - - - - - - - - - - - - - - - - - - - - - - - - - -

_____

_____

- - - - - - - - - - - - - - - - - - - - - - - - - - - - - -

_____

# Spell Short u Words

Some words follow a spelling pattern. **Short u** is often spelled **u**, as in **bug**. Other words do not follow a pattern. You must remember how to spell them.

**MY TURN** Read and spell the short **u** words. Then spell the My Words to Know words.

| Spelling Words | | | |
|---|---|---|---|
| bug | hug | tug | dug |

**Short u**

bug

| My Words to Know | |
|---|---|
| to | with |

# Sentences with Nouns, Verbs, and Adjectives

**Sentences** tell complete ideas. They have nouns, verbs, and sometimes they have adjectives. **Nouns** name people, animals, or things. **Verbs** tell about a noun. **Adjectives** describe nouns.

**MY TURN** Read the sentences. Edit the draft by adding a sentence that has a noun, a verb, and an adjective.

Sam makes a map. The map has many streets.

Sam

**My Learning Goal**

I can write a story.

# Choose a Book to Publish

Choose something you wrote that you want to publish, or share.

**MY TURN** Write a title for your book.

_____

- - - - - - - - - - - - - - - - - - - - - - - - - - - - - - - - - - - -

_____

# Edit for Illustrations and Words

**MY TURN** Use the chart to help you edit your writing. Check **yes** or **no**.

|  | Yes | No |
|---|---|---|
| **Are my illustrations complete?** | ○ | ○ |
| **Are there details in the words?** | ○ | ○ |

**TURN and TALK** What might you want to add or change before you publish your writing?

# How to Celebrate

It's time to celebrate your writing.

Follow the rules for speaking and listening.

1. Speak clearly when it is your turn.

2. Ask questions if you do not understand.

3. Listen to others.

4. Make appropriate comments.

**TURN and TALK** Introduce yourself to your partner. Tell about your experience writing. Then introduce each other to the group.

# Assessment

 **MY TURN** Mark **yes** or **no** for each statement.

| I know . . . | Yes | No |
| --- | --- | --- |
| who authors are and what they do. | | |
| what good writers do. | | |
| Writing Workshop steps. | | |
| what digital tools I can use. | | |
| the features of a fiction book. | | |
| the features of a nonfiction book. | | |
| how to add details to illustrations. | | |
| how to add details to words. | | |
| how to celebrate my writing. | | |

**TURN and TALK** Talk about things you need to do to strengthen your writing.

Read Together

UNIT THEME

# My Neighborhood

 **TURN** and **TALK**

Find a word from each text that names something in a neighborhood. Write the word by the text.

**WEEK 3** Look Both Ways!

_____
- - - - - - - - - - - - - - -
_____

BOOK CLUB

**WEEK 2** from **Henry on Wheels**

_____
- - - - - - - - - - - - - - -
_____

BOOK CLUB

**WEEK 1** The Blackout

_____
- - - - - - - - - - - - - - -
_____

**BOOK CLUB**

## Garden Party and Click, Clack, Click!

_____

- - - - - - - - - - - - - - - -

_____

**BOOK CLUB**

## Making a Map

_____

- - - - - - - - - - - - - - - -

_____

## Essential Question

**MY TURN**

What is a neighborhood?

**BOOK CLUB**

### Project

Now it's time to apply what you learned about neighborhoods in your **WEEK 6 PROJECT:** People in My Neighborhood.

# Initial Sounds

 **SEE and SAY** Say the name of each picture.
Listen to the beginning sound of each word.
Say the sound at the beginning of each word.

## Qu, qu

The letters **qu** together make the sound
at the beginning of the word **quit**.

**MY TURN** Read the word.

# Qu, qu

 **TURN** *and* **TALK** Read these sentences with a partner.

 **Will Quinn quit?**

 **Quinn will not quit.**

 **MY TURN** Say each picture name. Write the letters that stand for the beginning sound of each picture name.

quilt

___een

 **TURN** *and* **TALK** Tell your partner a sentence with a **qu** word.

# Qu, qu

**MY TURN** Point to the words as you listen to these sentences. <u>Underline</u> the words with the **kw** sound.

Can <u>Quinn</u> do the quiz?

Can Bess do the quiz?

They have one pen.

Will they quit the quiz?

The letters **qu** stand for the **kw** sound.

**MY TURN** Write a sentence about Quinn.

Quinn

Read Together

# Spell Words with Qu, qu

The sound **kw** is spelled **qu**.

**MY TURN** Look at the spelling patterns to sort and write the words. Then spell the My Words to Know words.

| Spelling Words | | | |
|---|---|---|---|
| quit | bit | quill | will |

**-it**

quit

**-ill**

**My Words to Know**

| where | go |
|---|---|

**Read Together**

# Initial and Final Sounds

 **SEE and SAY** Say what the bee does in the first picture. Listen to the ending sound. Name the other pictures. Listen to the beginning sounds.

## Vv, Yy, Zz

The letter **v** has the **v** sound in **vet**.

The letter **y** has the **y** sound in **yak**.

The letter **z** has the **z** sound in **zip**.

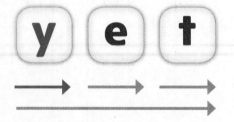 **MY TURN** Read these words.

v a n          y e t

# My Words to Know

Some words you must remember and practice.

**MY TURN** Read these words.

| go | me | for | here | where |
|----|-----|-----|------|-------|

**MY TURN** Use words from the box to complete the sentences. Then read the sentences.

1. Where is Zak?

2. He is _____ .

3. Zak will _____ to the vet

   with _____ .

4. The tag is _____ Zak.

# Vv, Yy, Zz

**TURN and TALK** Read these words with a partner.

| | | |
|---|---|---|
| **yum** | **vet** | **zap** |

| | | |
|---|---|---|
| **van** | **zag** | **yet** |

**MY TURN** Say each picture name.
Write the letter **v**, **y**, or **z** to make the words.
Read the words.

y ak

qui

ip

an

# Vv, Yy, Zz

**MY TURN** Write a sentence about two friends named Viv and Yaz. Then draw a picture of Viv and Yaz.

Viv and Yaz

# Quinn the Vet

AUDIO

Audio with Highlighting

 ANNOTATE

I am Quinn the vet.

The van is for me.

I will go to see a pet.

Read the title and the story. Underline the three words with the **v** sound.

Where is Zak?

Here he is!

Yip! Yap!

Quit that, Zak!

Highlight the two words with the **y** sound and the word with the **kw** sound.

Is <u>Zak</u> well?

Yes, he is.

Look at him zip by!

<u>Underline</u> the two words that begin
with the **z** sound.

# People in My Neighborhood

## Activity

Choose a worker in your neighborhood and explain what he or she does.

### RESEARCH

**Let's Read!**
This week you will read three articles about neighborhoods.

**1** Workers in the Neighborhood

**2** Walking to School

**3** All Aboard the Bus

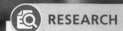 **COLLABORATE** Talk about neighborhood workers. Think of two questions to research.

# Use Academic Words

**COLLABORATE** You learned many new academic words in this unit. Use the words to talk about the picture with a partner.

## Neighborhood Worker Research Plan

**Day 1** List two questions.

**Day 2** Research a neighborhood worker.

**Day 3** Write an informational text.

**Day 4** Revise and edit your text.

**Day 5** Present your informational text.

# Inform Your Readers

Some authors write to inform readers about a topic. When reading informational text, look for a main, or central, idea and details.

 **COLLABORATE** Read "Walking to School" with a partner. Then fill in the chart.

## Main Idea

## Details

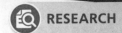 RESEARCH

# Check It Out!

My neighborhood worker is

_____

-----------------------------------------

_____.

Two questions about my neighborhood worker are

_____

1. _____

_____

2. _____

**COLLABORATE** (Circle) the source where you will look for information to answer your questions.

**books**

**librarian**

# Informational Text

Informational texts include a main idea and details. The details tell more about the main idea.

**Main Idea**

One neighborhood worker is a dad. A dad takes his children to school. He can play with them. He can make dinner for them. Dads have an important job in the neighborhood.

**Details**

# Identify Relevant Sources 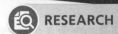 RESEARCH

**COLLABORATE** Before you use a book for research, make sure it is about your topic. Books about your topic will help you answer your questions. You can gather, or collect, books that will help you answer your questions. Follow these steps:

**1.** Read the title.

**2.** Look at the cover and pictures.

**3.** Use what you see to decide if the book is about your topic.

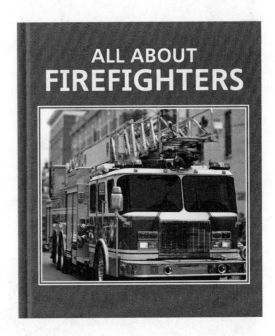

**COLLABORATE** With a partner, find a source for your topic. Write the title of the book.

Book title: _____

# Picture This!

You can use pictures to help your readers see more details about your topic.

Often, pictures can tell more than words!

**COLLABORATE** With a partner, draw a life-size picture of the worker you chose. Include specific details that develop your ideas.

# Revise

**COLLABORATE** Read your informational text to your partner. Circle **yes** or **no**.

| Did you need to | | |
|---|---|---|
| revise the main idea? | yes | no |
| add details to the words? | yes | no |
| add details to the picture? | yes | no |

# Edit

**COLLABORATE** Read your informational text again.

**Check for**

☐ nouns

☐ verbs

☐ adjectives

# Share

 **COLLABORATE** Share your informational text.

Follow these rules for **speaking and listening.**

- Listen actively.
- Share ideas about the topic.
- Speak clearly.

# Reflect

 **MY TURN** Complete the sentences.

The source that helped me most is

_____

_____

_____

_____

The hardest part of research is

_____

_____

_____

_____

# Reflect on Your Goals

Look back at your unit goals. Use a different color to rate yourself again.

**MY TURN** Complete the sentences.

# Reflect on Your Reading

The hardest text to read from this unit is

_____

_____

# Reflect on Your Writing

The writing I like best from this unit is

_____

_____

# How to Use a Picture Dictionary

You can use a picture dictionary to find words. The words are grouped into topics. The topic of this picture dictionary is **locations**. Look at the pictures, and try to read the words. The pictures will help you understand the meanings of the words.

> This is a picture of the word.

## fire station

> This is the word you are learning.

**TURN and TALK** Find the word **school** in the picture dictionary. Use the word in sentences to show you understand what the word means.

## Locations

grocery store

police station

hospital

school

library

train station

park

# How to Use a Glossary

A glossary can help you find the meanings of words you do not know. The words in a glossary are in alphabetical, or ABC, order. Guide words at the top of the pages can help you find words.

> All words that begin with the letter S will be after Ss.

> The word is in dark type.

**Ss**　　　　**sand** **Sand** is tiny grains of broken rock.

> This sentence will help you understand what the word means.

**MY TURN** Find the word **library** in the glossary. Draw a picture of what the word means.

# Bb

**block**  A **block** is the area in a city or town enclosed by four streets.

**buildings**  **Buildings** are structures with walls and roofs where people do activities.

# Cc

**check**  When you **check** something, you examine it to see if it is correct, working properly, and so on.

**corner**  A **corner** is the place where two streets meet.

**crosswalk**  A **crosswalk** is an area marked by lines that is used by people walking across the street.

# Gg

**group**  A **group** is a number of people or things together.

**guard**  A **guard** is a person who protects or watches. A crossing guard protects and watches people cross the street safely.

# Hh

**help**  To **help** means to give or do what is needed or useful.

# Jj

**join**  When you **join**, you become a member of some kind of group.

# Ll

**left**  **Left** is the opposite of right. Left is the direction toward the bold word.

**library** A **library** is a room or building where books and other materials are for borrowing. People can borrow magazines, videos, and music too.

**listen** When you **listen**, you try to hear something or someone.

## Mm

**meet** When people **meet**, they get together at a certain time or place.

**mutters** When a person **mutters**, he or she mumbles.

## Pp

**plant** When you **plant**, you put something in the ground so it can grow.

# Qq

**quiet** When you are **quiet**, you do not make a sound.

# Rr

**right** **Right** is the opposite of left. Right is the direction toward the next page.

# Ss

**sand** **Sand** is tiny grains of broken rock.

**school** A **school** is a place where people learn things in a group.

**settle** When you **settle**, you set up a new place to live.

**stores** **Stores** are places where people can buy things.

**street** A **street** is a road in a city or town.

# Tt

**type** A **type** is a kind, sort, or group that is alike in some way.

# Vv

**various** **Various** means different from one another.

## Text

### HarperCollins Publishers

*Everything Goes: Henry on Wheels* by Brian Biggs. Copyright ©2013 by Brian Biggs. Used by permission of HarperCollins Publishers.

### Photographs

Photo locators denoted as follows  Top (T), Center (C), Bottom (B), Left (L), Right (R), Background (Bkgd)

4 Image Sources/Getty Images; 6 (Bkgd) RoschetzkyProductions/Shutterstock, (BL) Elenathewise/123RF; 7 Image Sources/Getty Images; 11 Jeremy Woodhouse/Blend Images/ Getty Images; 12 (B) Divedog/Shutterstock, (CR) EvgeniiAnd/Shutterstock; 13 Effe45/ Shutterstock; 14 (BC) Testing/Shutterstock, (BL) Hugh Lansdown/Shutterstock, (BR) Eric Isselee/Shutterstock, (CR) Stephen VanHorn/ Shutterstock, (TC) Coprid/Shutterstock, (TL) Axel Bueckert/Shutterstock, (TR) Apopium/Fotolia; 15 (BL) Axel Bueckert/ Shutterstock, (BR) Lucadp/Shutterstock, (CL) Testing/Shutterstock, (CR) Hugh Lansdown/ Shutterstock; 16 (CL) KKulikov/Shutterstock, (CR) Apopium/Fotolia, (TL) Stephen VanHorn/ Shutterstock, (TR) Coprid/Shutterstock; 17 (C) Stephen VanHorn/Shutterstock, (CL) Lakov Filimonov/Shutterstock, (CR) Shutterstock; 19 Photographee/Shutterstock; 20 (CL) Lucadp/ Shutterstock, (CR) Toey Toey/Shutterstock, (TL) Eurobanks/Shutterstock, (TR) Claudio Divizia/ Shutterstock; 50 (B) Cah Yati/Shutterstock, (BC) Fernando Kazuo/Shutterstock, (C) Team Oktopus/Shutterstock, (CL) Leosapiens/ Shutterstock, (CR) KittyVector/Shutterstock, (Bkgd) Avelkrieg/123RF; 51 (BL) Oxanakot/ Shutterstock, (BC) Andrii Bezvershenko/ Shutterstock, (B) Avian/Shutterstock, (C) TatiVasko/Shutterstock, (T) Trifonenkolvan/ Shutterstock; 52 (TC) HstrongART/Shutterstock, (TR) Tsekhmister/Shutterstock; 53 (BR) Dave Pot/Shutterstock, (CL) Luis Molinero/ Shutterstock, (CR) Elena Elisseeva/Shutterstock; 54 Veronica Louro/Shutterstock; 55 (C) Carsten Reisinger/Shutterstock, (CL) Alena Brozova/ Shutterstock, (CR) Terekhov Igor/Shutterstock; 58 (CR) Axel Bueckert/Shutterstock, (TL) Stephen VanHorn/Shutterstock, (TR) KKulikov/ Shutterstock; 62 Zstock/Shutterstock; 64 Photograph by Sacha Adorno; 94 Mark_KA/ Shutterstock; 96 (Bkgd) Suwatsilp Sooksang/ Shutterstock, (C) Tyler Olson/Shutterstock; 97 (CL) Pamela Au/Shutterstock, (CR) Pamela Au/ Shutterstock; 98 (CR) Italika/Shutterstock, (TC) Pim Leijen/Shutterstock, (TL) Africa Studio/ Shutterstock, (TR) Josefauer/Shutterstock; 99 (BL) Italika/Shutterstock, (CL) Mates/ Shutterstock, (CR) Indigolotos/Shutterstock, (BR) Lifes All White/Alamy Stock Photo; 101 (TC) Jacek Fulawka/Shutterstock, (TL) Galushko Sergey/Shutterstock, (TR) BBA Photography/ Shutterstock; 104 (BL) BillionPhoto/ Shutterstock, (TL) Apopium/Fotolia; 111 Image Sources/Getty Images; 112 Pitchayarat Chootai/ Shutterstock; 113 Indeed/Getty Images; 114 Kali9/iStock/Getty Images Plus/Getty Images; 115 Kali9/iStock/Getty Images Plus/Getty Images; 116 (BL) Dean Hammel/Shutterstock, (TR) Blickwinkel/Alamy Stock Photo; 117 Peter Titmuss/Alamy Stock Photo; 118 Fotog/Getty Images; 119 (T) Image Source/Getty Images, (B) Fotog/Getty Images; 120 (T) Pitchayarat Chootai/Shutterstock, (B) Kali9/iStock/Getty Images Plus/Getty Images; 124 Golden Pixels LLC/Shutterstock; 128 Alinute Silzeviciute/ Shutterstock; 132 (B) Thomas Marchessault/ Alamy Stock Photo, (T) Wavebreakmedia/ Shutterstock; 133 Rawpixel/Shutterstock; 134 (TC) Terekhov Igor/Shutterstock, (TL) Morenina/Shutterstock, (TR) 123RF; 135 (BL) Jennifer Huls/123RF, (BR) Morenina/ Shutterstock, (CL) Maxriesgo/Shutterstock, (CR) Terekhov Igor/Shutterstock; 137 (TC) Josefauer/ Shutterstock, (TL) Coprid/Shutterstock, (TR) Eric Isselee/Shutterstock; 140 (TC) Discpicture/ Shutterstock, (TL) Ananaline/Shutterstock, (TR) Coprid/Shutterstock; 170 Dvoevnore/ Shutterstock; 174 (Bkgd) PK.Inspiration_06/ Shutterstock, (B) TDKvisuals/Shutterstock; 175 Christian Lagerek/Shutterstock; 176 (TC) 123RF, (TR) Chudtsankov/123RF; 177 (BL) LifetimeStock/Shutterstock, (BR) Johnfoto18/ Shutterstock, (CL) Chudtsankov/123RF, (CR) 123RF; 178 (BR) Imstock/Shutterstock, (CL) Chudtsankov/123RF, (CR) Higyou/Shutterstock; 179 (CL) Kiri11/Shutterstock, (CR) Jelena Aloskina/Shutterstock, (TL) Bezmaski/ Shutterstock, (TR) Hellen Grig/Shutterstock; 182 (L) LifetimeStock/Shutterstock, (R) Hellen Grig/Shutterstock; 210 (Bkgd) 123RF, (TR) Image Sources/Getty Images; 211 Syda Productions/Shutterstock; 212 (TC) Poter_N/ Shutterstock, (TL) Jackhollingsworth/ Shutterstock, (TR) Georgios Kollidas/ Shutterstock; 213 (L) Hurst Photo/Shutterstock, (R) Poter_N/Shutterstock; 216 (TCL) Bright/ Shutterstock, (TCR) Nerthuz/Shutterstock,

(TL) 123RF, (TR) Nico Smit/123RF; **218** (BL) Africa Studio/Shutterstock, (BR) Nerthuz/Shutterstock, (CL) Eric Isselee/Shutterstock, (CR) Takasu/Shutterstock; **224** Syda Productions/Shutterstock; **227** (BL) Africa Studio/Shutterstock, (BR) Tyler Olson/Shutterstock; **229** (CR) Jennifer Vinciguerra/Shutterstock, (R) Udovichenko/Shutterstock; **234** Michael G Meyer/iStock/Getty Images Plus/Getty Images; **235** (hospital) Peter Titmuss/Alamy Stock Photo, (library) Sylvie Bouchard/Shutterstock, (park) Trong Nguyen/Shutterstock, (train station) Trevor Smith/Alamy Stock Photo, (police station) Images-USA/Alamy Stock Photo, (grocery store) Kondor83/Shutterstock, (school) Jack Schiffer/Shutterstock; **237** Pitchayarat Chootai/Shutterstock; **238** Kali9/iStock/Getty Images Plus/Getty Images; **239** (B) G-stockstudio/Shutterstock, (T) Golden Pixels LLC/Shutterstock; **240** Coprid/123RF; **241** (B) Zhu Difeng/Shutterstock, (T) MTaira/Shutterstock.

### Illustrations

**Unit 1: 12** André Jolicoeur; **21–23, 105–107, 220–223** Benedetta Capriotti; **25, 109** Chris Vallo; **27–38, 40, 46** Maxime Lebrun; **42, 48, 94, 166, 171, 230** Tim Johnson; **59–61, 183–185** Juliana Motzko; **63, 145, 187** Ken Bowser; **65–84** Simon Abbott; **141–143** Genie Espinosa; **147–153** Debbie Palen; **155–161** Peter Francis; **189–198, 200** Valentina Belloni

# NOTES